THIS BOOK BELONGS TO

....

....

D1468834

BALLANTINE BOOKS BY DEBBIE MACOMBER

Cottage by the Sea

Debbie Macomber's Table

Any Dream Will Do

If Not for You

The World of Debbie Macomber: Come Home to Color

A Girl's Guide to Moving On

Last One Home

ROSE HARBOR INN

Sweet Tomorrows

Silver Linings

Love Letters

Rose Harbor in Bloom

The Inn at Rose Harbor

BLOSSOM STREET

Blossom Street Brides

Starting Now

CHRISTMAS NOVELS

Alaskan Holiday

Merry and Bright

Twelve Days of Christmas

Dashing Through the Snow

Mr. Miracle

Starry Night

Angels at the Table

For a complete list of books by Debbie Macomber,
visit her website at debbiemacomber.com.

Be a Blessing

Be a Blessing

A Journal for Cultivating Kindness,
Joy, and Inspiration

DEBBIE MACOMBER

Ballantine Books
New York

Published in the United States by Ballantine Books,
an imprint of Random House, a division of
Penguin Random House LLC, New York.

BALLANTINE and the HOUSE colophon are registered
trademarks of Penguin Random House LLC.

Hardback ISBN 978-0-399-18142-9

Printed in China on acid-free paper

randomhousebooks.com

2 4 6 8 9 7 5 3 1

First Edition

Designed by Debbie Glasserman

To

Ashley Hayes

and

Adele LaCombe

Who inspired and encouraged
me through this book

The one thing you
have that nobody else
has is you. Your voice, your
mind, your story, your vision.
So, write and draw and
build and play and dance
and live as only you can.

NEIL GAIMAN

Journaling helps me deal with all that life throws at me, both joys and sorrows. To write my innermost thoughts with pen and paper (yes, the old-fashioned way!) is a priority, whether it be the highlights of my day, things that make me thankful, or prayers I lift to God, to name only a few. I've journaled my entire life and have reaped the rewards from this daily discipline. My hope is that by using this journal, you will also see the benefits of putting a pen to paper, of taking a thoughtful look at your life as you may never have done before.

This is a journal about planting a garden—a garden in which these fruits are grown: love, joy, peace, patience, kindness, goodness, faithfulness, gentleness, and self-control. Along the way, we'll discuss weeding, watering, and fertilizing your own soul, so that you can be a blessing to others while harvesting wonderful benefits for yourself.

I'm humbled to have you join me in this process of looking inside your heart and gardening your soul. Grab your gardening tools— your pens and coloring utensils—and let's dig in!

Warmly,

Debbie

LET'S GET STARTED BY LOOKING AT OUR GARDEN:
WHAT DOES THE PLOT OR PIECE OF SOIL THAT IS
IN FRONT OF YOU LOOK LIKE RIGHT NOW?

....

....

....

....

....

....

....

....

....

....

....

....

....

WHERE ARE YOU IN LIFE AT THIS MOMENT IN TIME,
AS YOU START THIS JOURNALING PROCESS WITH ME?

WHO INSPIRES OR ENCOURAGES YOU?

LIST THE THINGS THAT CAUSE
YOU STRESS IN YOUR DAILY LIFE.

☀ ....

☀ ....

☀ ....

☀ ....

☀ ....

☀ ....

☀ ....

☀ ....

☀ ....

☀ ....

☀ ....

☀ ....

☀ ....

☀ ....

☀ ....

To whom
AND TO
what
DO YOU TURN IN TIMES OF
STRESS?

....

....

....

....

....

....

....

THE FRUITS OF THE SPIRIT

Love

Joy

Peace

ARE GOD'S GIFT TO US.

Patience

Kindness

Goodness

Faithfulness

Gentleness

Self-control

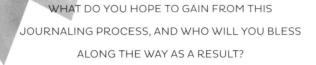

WHAT DO YOU HOPE TO GAIN FROM THIS
JOURNALING PROCESS, AND WHO WILL YOU BLESS
ALONG THE WAY AS A RESULT?

....

....

....

....

....

....

....

....

....

....

....

....

....

....

....

What are your favorite quotes that inspire you?

I've been planting a vegetable garden since I was a newlywed and a mother of young children. There's something so satisfying about growing food for yourself and your family. From looking at the seed catalogs, to planting, watering, weeding, fertilizing, and harvesting—the entire process of having my own garden has given me a deep sense of doing something positive for myself and for those I love.

Another garden I've worked on through the years is my own personal garden of life, in which I focus on self-growth, nurturing, and feeding my soul to live a more abundant and fruitful life.

THINK OF **FIVE** THINGS IN YOUR *life*
THAT YOU WANT TO
nourish, ENRICH, OR *improve.*

1. ....
2. ....
3. ....
4. ....
5. ....

Plant a garden in the
Eden of my soul.
Awaken the springtime blossoms
hidden in winter darkness.

ROBIN JONES GUNN

I'm a huge proponent of making lists. In fact, one of my own personal commandments is: "Thou shall not be listless." And I'm not just talking about grocery lists. I make a list of all the chapters of a new book before I even put my fingers to the keyboard, for example. I have an old and fading list of all my dreams written on a light-blue notepad, which includes family goals and personal goals, as well as hopes for my career. I have a list of places where I want to go and people who I want to meet.

Having a list is much like the very beginnings of a garden: the seeds that you plant in the soil for your much-anticipated harvest.

HERE'S MY CHALLENGE TO YOU: START A LIST!
WHAT SEEDS ARE YOU WILLING TO PLANT IN THE RICH SOIL
OF YOUR MIND? WHAT ARE *YOUR* HOPES, DREAMS, AND GOALS
FOR YOUR FAMILY, YOURSELF, AND YOUR CAREER?

HOPES

_____
_____
_____
_____
_____
_____
_____
_____
_____
_____

DREAMS

_____
_____
_____
_____
_____
_____
_____
_____
_____

GOALS

_____
_____
_____
_____
_____
_____
_____
_____
_____
_____
_____

YOU DON'T HAVE TO BE RICH OR HAVE A LOT
OF FREE TIME TO BE A BLESSING TO THOSE IN YOUR LIFE.
THINK OF SOME WAYS YOU CAN GIVE SIMPLE, EVERYDAY
BLESSINGS TO PEOPLE YOU LOVE.

....

....

....

....

....

....

....

....

SUPPORT COMPLIMENT

HELP LOVE

FRIENDSHIP PRAISE

We all have areas in our lives covered with weeds and thorny vines that need to be cleared. Places to be tilled and the soil enriched before we can even start planting the seeds. A healthy lifestyle is a constant area of focus for me. Before we can live that abundant life, be a blessing to others, and reap the rewards, some of us need to do some serious weeding!

WHAT WEEDS DO YOU NEED TO CLEAR OUT OF YOUR LIFE?

WHAT'S KEEPING YOU FROM HAVING A BOUNTIFUL LIFE?

BE
✳A✳
BLESSING

✳

Three simple words,
but what a profound impact we
experience when we act on them.

TAKING GOOD CARE OF A GARDEN

REQUIRES A GOOD SET OF TOOLS.

For instance, a sturdy shovel will not only get deep, ingrained roots out of your garden, but it also may find some treasure! A tiller will turn up the soil, giving rise to fresh ideas and dreams. A pruner trims away excess; in our own lives, it may cut away hurts, resentments, and distractions. A hoe will dig up pesky weeds that are too hard to pull out by hand and help to rid you of the self-doubt and criticism from others that hold you back. A good hose—we all need precious water to refresh our spirits and encourage growth.

IT IS TIME TO ASSEMBLE YOUR TOOLS.

HOW WILL YOU USE THEM?

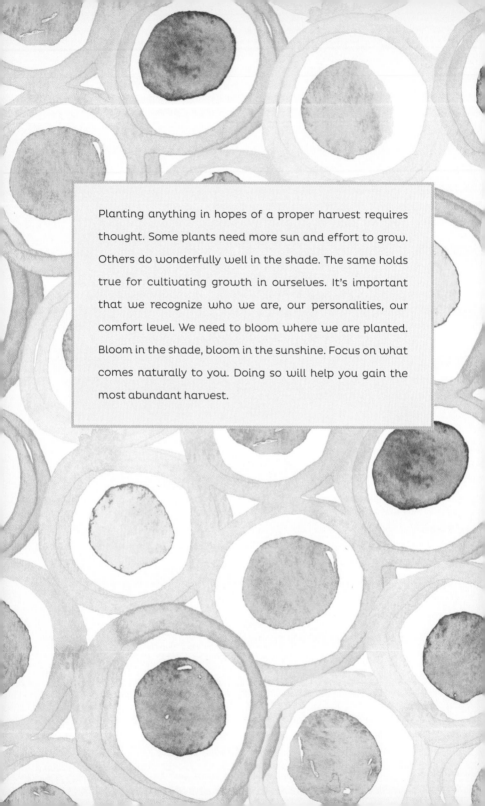

Planting anything in hopes of a proper harvest requires thought. Some plants need more sun and effort to grow. Others do wonderfully well in the shade. The same holds true for cultivating growth in ourselves. It's important that we recognize who we are, our personalities, our comfort level. We need to bloom where we are planted. Bloom in the shade, bloom in the sunshine. Focus on what comes naturally to you. Doing so will help you gain the most abundant harvest.

START
where you
STAND,
and work
WITH WHATEVER
TOOLS
you may have
at your
COMMAND.

NAPOLEON HILL

TIME TO PLAN YOUR GARDEN! WHAT DO YOU PLAN TO GROW
AND CULTIVATE IN THIS SEASON OF LIFE?

....

....

....

....

....

....

....

....

....

....

What is the most
rigorous law of our being?

GROWTH.

MARK TWAIN

I was five years into my pursuit of selling a manuscript. I'd written a total of four books. When those were rejected, I felt as if the seeds of my dreams had died in the soil I had so carefully prepared and tilled.

But I continued to water that dream, hoping to see at least *one* of those first four books break through the ground with a tender shot. I thought it had happened when I was given the opportunity of a lifetime: An editor was attending the same conference as me and had agreed to review my manuscript. I felt like I had been given a chance to meet the Pope!

Well, to say she didn't like my story would be an understatement. When I offered to rewrite it for her, she looked at me with sympathetic eyes, and suggested the best place for my story was the garbage. Five years. Four completed manuscripts. The most fitting place for my dreams was a *garbage can*? If I had given up, I would have had a total of four stories, and one full garbage can! I wouldn't have had a fruitful and satisfying career.

ARE THERE AREAS IN YOUR LIFE
THAT YOU SHOULDN'T GIVE UP ON?

What other people label or might try to call failure I have learned is just God's way of pointing you in a new direction.

OPRAH WINFREY

SOMETIMES FLOWERS OR PLANTS MUST
GROW THROUGH HARD SOIL.

Write about a time you were trying to plant a garden and you
had to work the soil extra hard before the flowers would grow.

....

....

....

....

....

....

....

....

....

....

....

....

....

....

....

....

Leave your
stepping stones
behind,
something calls
for you.

BOB DYLAN

WHAT STEPS WILL YOU TAKE TO
ACCOMPLISH YOUR GOALS?

I've struggled with weight issues my entire life. My mother was a beautiful, slender woman who never weighed more than 120 pounds. For her to have an overweight daughter was embarrassing. From the time I was in third grade, she had me on a diet, which damaged my self-image. The irony is that in looking back at my childhood photos, I looked completely normal. Before, I saw all my flaws. Now I am able to see myself as I really was—a smiling, cute kid.

WHO YOU ARE NOW. PASTE IN A PICTURE OF
YOURSELF AND WRITE ABOUT WHO YOU ARE.

WHO DO YOU WANT TO BE? PASTE IN A PICTURE OF SOMEONE
YOU ADMIRE. WRITE ABOUT ALL THE THINGS YOU ASPIRE TO BE.

Remember, beauty comes from within first and foremost.

IS IT DIFFICULT TO LOVE YOURSELF?

REFLECT ON A TIME YOU WERE HARD ON YOURSELF.

WAS IT HELPFUL? HOW DO YOU FEEL NOW?

....

....

....

....

....

....

....

....

....

....

....

....

....

....

....

The oddest-looking plant sprung up in my garden. It didn't look like a weed. The leaves and sprout resembled an onion. Only I hadn't planted any onions in that section of my vegetable garden. I left it alone to see what would become of it, although I was tempted to uproot it any number of times. This odd plant, this weed, as it turned out, was garlic. And that garlic was wonderful. Some of the oddest-looking plants in life aren't always weeds. It takes time and patience to discern what really is a weed, and what may become something good that's been planted in our lives.

WHAT ARE THE WEEDS YOU HAVE IN YOUR LIFE THAT OTHERS
MIGHT SEE AS BUDS WAITING TO BLOOM INTO FLOWERS?

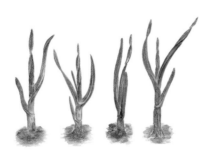

Fill these leaves with
all the qualities you
L·O·V·E
about yourself.

Our eyes generally see the things we
don't like about ourselves first, but if we focus
we can find the beauty.

YOU *demonstrate* **love** *by giving it* **unconditionally** TO YOURSELF.

PAUL FERRINI

Not all goals or dreams will be beautiful, and that's okay. As long as I could remember, I've always wanted to play the piano. My parents invested in one and paid for me to have lessons. I honestly tried but found it difficult. I couldn't seem to get my fingers to do what I wanted them to. Growing discouraged, I quit. Later, as an adult, I tried again. Wayne bought me another piano, and again, I experienced the same difficulty. I realized that although I wanted to play the piano, that wasn't where my talent or strength lay. I'm too dyslexic!

WRITE ABOUT

GOALS

> OR <

experiences

THAT YOU CAN

LET GO OF,

THAT MAY NOT BE THE RIGHT

FIT

for your garden.

·····

·····

·····

·····

·····

·····

Some people "go" through life;
others "grow" through life.

ROBERT HOLDEN

One aspect of loving yourself is recognizing and acknowledging all the small details in life that make you happy. We often refer to this as "filling our cup," but in this journal we are going to fill our watering pail. Take an audit of your life and evaluate the things that make you most fulfilled.

THINGS THAT
FULFILL MY LIFE

My cup
runneth
over.

PSALMS 23:5

If anyone were to read the journals I've kept over the years, they would find them exceedingly dull. I write about my day, my activities, my family and friends, my knitting projects, and even new recipes I find and hope to try. Yet in between the lines of these pages is me. What's most important in my life. What has impacted me. It's through the expressions of my ordinary daily reminiscences that I've learned to know myself. When I look back, I can see the emotion buried underneath the words. Joy. Depression. Sadness. Excitement. All within a single page, hidden in the ordinary.

SPEND TIME ALONE. FOR SOME IT SOUNDS IMPOSSIBLE.
BUT MY CHALLENGE TO YOU IS TO FIND THAT TIME. GET UP
EARLY BEFORE EVERYONE ELSE, IF YOU MUST, LIKE I DO.
THIS PRACTICE CAN BE VERY BENEFICIAL IN SELF-GROWTH.
WHAT WILL YOU DO WITH THAT TIME?

Get enough sleep

Write in a journal

Spend time with animals

Take a walk

eat BREAKFAST

COOK at Home

Read more Books

START each day with a WORKOUT

ME TIME

monday	tuesday	wednesday

KEEP TRACK OF WAYS YOU SPEND TIME ON YOURSELF FOR A
WEEK. DEVOTE "ME TIME" TO GETTING TO KNOW YOUR
HEART, MIND, AND SOUL.

thursday   friday   saturday   sunday

Journaling and spending time by myself are my ways of staying in touch with my feelings, which is sometimes difficult. I don't believe I'm alone in this. It's all too easy to ignore pain, hoping it will go away. A toothache, a sore knee. We opt to put up with our physical ailments instead of doing what's needed for them. It's the same with our emotional injuries. It helps me to ask myself what I am really feeling, and then, if I'm willing, to acknowledge and deal with it.

I enjoy knitting, reading, cooking, and, it should come as no surprise, gardening. Spending time in my garden is one of my greatest joys.

WHEN YOU ARE ALONE, WHAT DO YOU ENJOY DOING MOST? WHAT DOES THAT TELL YOU ABOUT YOURSELF?

FILL THE LINES WITH A PLAN FOR THE MONTH OF THINGS
YOU CAN DO FOR YOURSELF. HERE ARE A FEW THINGS I WILL
PUT ON MY OWN LIST: EXERCISING,
HEALTHY EATING, KNITTING, RELAXING.

Love
Yourself

1 2 3 4 5 6 7 8 9 10 11 12

Monthly Tracker

3 14 15 16 17 18 19 20 21 22 23 24 25 26 27 28 29 30 31

WHO ARE THE **FIVE** MOST IMPORTANT
PEOPLE IN YOUR *life?*

1. ....

2. ....

3. ....

4. ....

5. ....

A friend once told me he was asked
to list the most important people in his life. To
him, that was simple. He named his wife and his
children and his special friends. The counselor
stopped him. Then asked the question that stayed
with my friend from that point forward.
Where are *you* on that list?

In life there is usually one compliment
we often hear from others that we won't let ourselves
accept. Our personal insecurities override in our brain the
reaction to a particular sentence of praise from another.

What is a compliment you need to focus on letting yourself
accept from others?

Sometimes it is hard to see yourself in a positive way.
It is difficult to observe the sun shining in your own world.
When I reflect on this, my strengths are being friendly,
meeting people and engaging with them, and
showing the world my genuine heart
for helping others.

Find joy in the ordinary.

MAX LUCADO

Joy has nothing to do with what's happening around me. Joy is being able to smile when my day is full of lemons; it gives me the ability to look beyond my frustrations and not let them get me down. Joy has a lot to do with my relationship with God and the trust I have in Him. A sign on my desk says it perfectly: *"Debbie, I have everything under control. Trust me. Jesus."* That, my friends, says it all—that's joy!

When
life
gives
you
lemons,
make
lemonade.

Being happy and experiencing true joy are often intermingled in our minds. It wasn't until the death of our son, Dale, that I understood the difference between happiness and joy. That season of grief and loss helped me define it. Happiness for me is a surface emotion. Laughing with friends, sharing a bowl of popcorn with Wayne, or watering my garden. Joy, on the other hand, comes from inside my soul and cannot be replicated. It's holding our newborn grandson in my arms; it's Wayne taking my hand in church and feeling his love surround me. Even in the darkest of times, wonderful lessons about life can be learned.

FOR YEARS I'VE KEPT A GRATITUDE JOURNAL.
EACH MORNING I LIST FIVE THINGS FOR WHICH I'M MOST
GRATEFUL. IT STARTS MY DAY ON A POSITIVE NOTE WITH AN
ATTITUDE OF GRATITUDE. BEING GRATEFUL
FILLS MY HEART WITH

The root of

joy

is gratefulness.

DAVID STEINDL-RAST

WHAT FILLS YOUR HEART WITH JOY?

(Remember to push past small things that make you happy.

Think about what brings you true joy.)

I get a kick out of what advertisers try to pass off as joy. Supposedly, a special brand of this or that will make all the difference in our lives, and we listen and sometimes accept it as truth. I mean, really, how often have any of us sat in a luxurious outdoor bathtub next to a loved one, looking at a beautiful sunset? We need to not let others determine what will make us happy, what will bring us joy.

Joy,
rather than happiness,
is the goal of life.

ROLLO MAY

HOW DO YOU MAKE SURE THAT YOUR JOY IS NOT DEPENDENT

ON OTHERS OR ON MATERIAL THINGS?

WHAT MOMENTS IN LIFE ARE EASY TO LET SLIP THROUGH YOUR
FINGERS WITHOUT RECOGNIZING THE JOY THAT THEY BRING?

I remember when our youngest son was born—our fourth child in five years. *What were we thinking?* I was on my third year of sleep deprivation and my mother had come to help with the newborn. As I breast-fed Dale, the other three youngsters crawled on my lap, wanting special time with me. My mother looked at me, shook her head, and told me that these would be the happiest days of my life. I stared back at her and said, "You mean it gets worse?"

What kept me sane in those days was creating fun, inventive ways to occupy our children. We had rainy-day picnics beneath the kitchen table. We had backward day, when I served dinner for breakfast and breakfast for dinner. I made up silly games they loved and read lots of bedtime stories.

I understand now what my mother meant; those were the seeds I planted in my children's lives. Seeds of memories and love.

HOW CAN YOU BE CREATIVE AND FIND

joy

IN A CRAZY BUSY TIME OF LIFE?

....

....

....

....

....

....

....

....

....

....

THE MAN WHO DIES WITH THE MOST TOYS WINS.

Or in my case the most yarn.

What does this statement mean to you?

All too often we look to material things to fill the deep holes inside us. These are actually rocks in our garden that need to be removed. We're looking for satisfaction and meaning in things rather than in relationships . . . relationships with ourselves, with our families, or with God.

WHAT ARE THE ROCKS YOU NEED
TO DIG OUT OF YOUR GARDEN?

WHAT IS GROWING IN YOUR LIFE RIGHT NOW?

Over the years I've learned that sometimes what seems to be a bitter disappointment in my life has turned out to be a blessing. At one time Wayne and I were forced to move because of an environmental situation. We left a home and community we loved and ended up in Port Orchard, which eventually became the basis of my Cedar Cove series. What appeared at first to be a total disaster ended up being a blessing.

LIKE HERBS SUCH AS MINT OR CHAMOMILE, THERE ARE
CIRCUMSTANCES IN LIFE THAT CAN CARRY A BITTER TONE
BUT IN THE END BECOME SWEET.
CAN YOU THINK OF SOMETHING IN YOUR
LIFE THAT IS BITTER BUT ALSO SWEET?

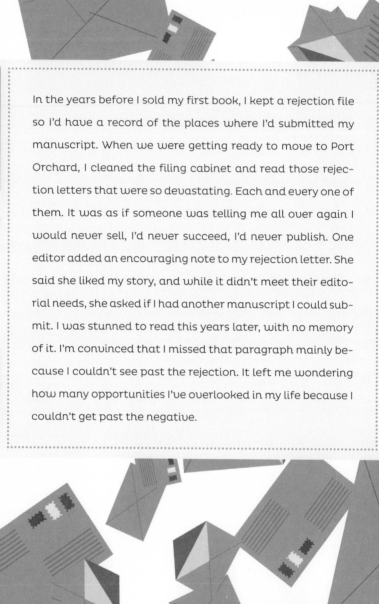

In the years before I sold my first book, I kept a rejection file so I'd have a record of the places where I'd submitted my manuscript. When we were getting ready to move to Port Orchard, I cleaned the filing cabinet and read those rejection letters that were so devastating. Each and every one of them. It was as if someone was telling me all over again I would never sell, I'd never succeed, I'd never publish. One editor added an encouraging note to my rejection letter. She said she liked my story, and while it didn't meet their editorial needs, she asked if I had another manuscript I could submit. I was stunned to read this years later, with no memory of it. I'm convinced that I missed that paragraph mainly because I couldn't see past the rejection. It left me wondering how many opportunities I've overlooked in my life because I couldn't get past the negative.

WHEN YOU FIND YOURSELF
IN A DROUGHT IN LIFE,
HOW DO YOU KEEP
YOURSELF GOING?

....

....

....

....

....

....

....

....

....

HOW DO YOU FIND JOY IN
THE SMALL MOMENTS
IN BETWEEN?

....

....

....

....

....

....

....

....

....

....

....

....

Peace is the beauty of life. It is sunshine. It is the smile of a child, the love of a mother, the joy of a father, the togetherness of a family. It is the advancement of man, the victory of a just cause, the triumph of truth.

MENACHEM BEGIN

Many years ago, a snowstorm hit the Seattle area after Christmas. Before the worst of it arrived, my parents, who had come to visit us, traveling from Yakima, decided to head home. Unfortunately, they didn't get out fast enough and were stopped in a small town when the mountain pass was closed due to avalanche warnings. They couldn't get back to us and we couldn't get to them. Both of my parents were elderly. I fretted and worried.

The local news channels were full of details about the hundreds of Christmas travelers trapped in this tiny town. Camera footage showed the shelters the city had provided. Lo and behold, there on TV were my mom and dad. Mom was leading the singing, and my dad sat at a table, playing cards. They made the best of a bad situation, and in the process met many new friends that they stayed in touch with after the storm.

Here I was, worrying about my parents, and they were perfectly safe. I've learned to turn to prayer in situations like this.

HOW DO YOU FIND PEACE IN TOUGH TIMES?

....

....

....

....

....

....

....

....

....

....

....

....

....

After the attacks on the twin towers in New York City, many parents wrote to Mr. Rogers, asking him how to explain to their children the horrific images filling the screens in their homes. Watching such terrible events, parents were worried about what their children would learn from this. Fred Rogers said, "Tell them to look for the helpers." When I heard this, I remember thinking what wise advice that was, and when I see tragedy now, things that are beyond human comprehension, I think of Fred Rogers's wisdom. Human nature has us focus on pain and horror. Instead, let your eyes and heart concentrate on those who are helping, rescuing, healing, comforting, and rebuilding.

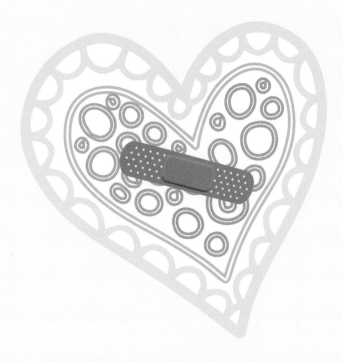

WHO ARE THE

helpers

IN YOUR

LIFE

THAT YOU

LOOK

TO IN A

difficult

TIME?

Often, despite all our best efforts, a section of our garden (or all of it) fails to produce the desired results. It might be a lack of sun; it could also be a bad season of pests. It's hard to put in all that effort and not see the results we'd hoped for. As discouraging and frustrating as it is, we need to replant, start over, begin again.

REFLECT ON A TIME WHEN YOU NEEDED A NEW BEGINNING.

Sometimes I'm working on a project or a story line and I must sit back and stop. I feel unsettled, and I eventually reach out to someone I trust for a second opinion.

Second opinions can often confirm or deny the inner turmoil we are feeling.

LIST 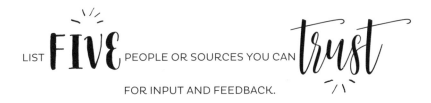 **FIVE** PEOPLE OR SOURCES YOU CAN *trust*

FOR INPUT AND FEEDBACK.

1. ....

2. ....

3. ....

4. ....

5. ....

*Peace
is not the
absence of
anything.
Real peace
is the
presence of
something
beautiful.*

PREM RAWAT

My parents grew up during the Great Depression. They lived in North and South Dakota during the dust bowl years. Their farms were devastated. Year after year of nothing but crop failures. No rain. No harvest. No hope. In spite of their faith, in spite of their prayers. With no other choice, they left the farms behind. They loaded up their families and all their earthly possessions and headed to Washington state, where they'd heard there were jobs. It felt as if God had turned a deaf ear to their prayers. God had other ideas, though. The move proved to be a good one as my parents met in Yakima, Washington. I believe we all experience those dust-bowl years in our lives, too, when we feel no one is listening, and our prayers go unanswered. But God has a plan. Find peace in knowing your rainbow is coming.

Undelivered
LETTERS
are like
unanswered
PRAYERS.
Both are a source of
FRUSTRATION!

But if you
persist,
believe,
move forward,
have hope and faith...
you will find
INNER PEACE.

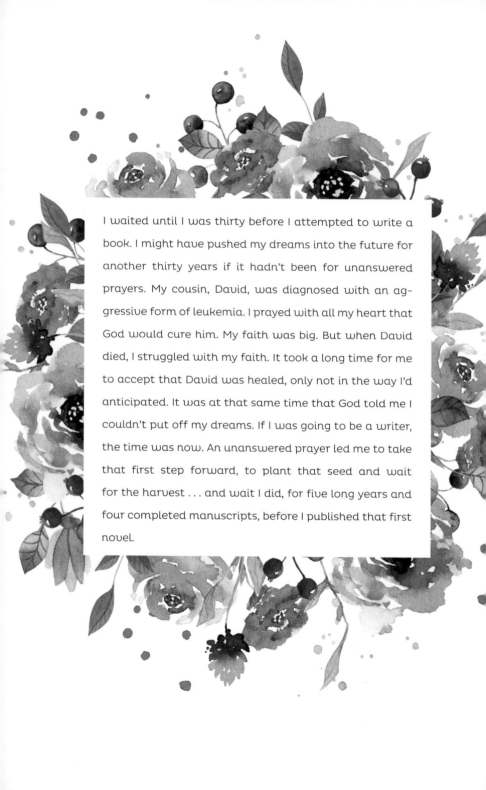

I waited until I was thirty before I attempted to write a book. I might have pushed my dreams into the future for another thirty years if it hadn't been for unanswered prayers. My cousin, David, was diagnosed with an aggressive form of leukemia. I prayed with all my heart that God would cure him. My faith was big. But when David died, I struggled with my faith. It took a long time for me to accept that David was healed, only not in the way I'd anticipated. It was at that same time that God told me I couldn't put off my dreams. If I was going to be a writer, the time was now. An unanswered prayer led me to take that first step forward, to plant that seed and wait for the harvest . . . and wait I did, for five long years and four completed manuscripts, before I published that first novel.

When we lay the soil of our hard lives open to the rain of grace and let joy penetrate our cracked and dry places, let joy soak into our broken skin and deep crevices, *life* grows. How can this not be the best thing for the world? For us?

ANN VOSKAMP

SOMETIMES THE STORY THAT IS CREATED FOR YOU IS BETTER
THAN ANY STORY YOU COULD HAVE WRITTEN FOR YOURSELF.

HAVE YOU HAD AN UNANSWERED PRAYER? OR HOPES AND
DREAMS THAT FELL FLAT? ONLY TO FIND OUT LATER THAT
THERE WAS SOMETHING BETTER IN STORE FOR YOU?

PATIENCE
is bitter,
BUT ITS
FRUIT
is
sweet.

JOHN CHARDIN

Sometimes we are forced to plant seeds in life and just wait. I wasn't very patient in my waiting process of getting published. I wasn't quietly tapping on doors and sending letters, I was throwing my entire body at those doors and flooding mailboxes with letters. What I didn't realize was that I was laying the foundation of my work habits, learning the value of revision, the willingness to get up and try again. All of these were tools that I would need in my career, developing a great deal of patience. If I had sold my first manuscript quickly, I would have never learned these valuable lessons.

Take rest; a field that has rested gives a bountiful crop.

OVID

WHAT ARE THE BEST WAYS TO FIND REST IN YOUR LIFE?

PERSISTENCE SOMETIMES HAS TO BE
BALANCED WITH PATIENCE.

WHAT ARE YOU BALANCING?

WHAT THINGS NEED PATIENCE?

WHAT THINGS NEED PERSISTENCE?

I have a rose garden that flourishes next to the house. It brings me great joy. My mother's name was Rose, and when she died, several friends gave me rosebushes in her memory. Each year when these roses bloom, I am reminded of the love of my friends and of the mother who patiently nourished my dreams.

INSTANT GRATIFICATION *takes too* LONG.

CARRIE FISHER

When we plant a seed, it goes into the ground and crumbles and then builds roots. Laying the groundwork and getting strong roots is everything for the life of that plant.

Waiting for your seeds to pop out of the ground takes a few weeks, but sometimes it feels like it takes forever. The time that seeds spend in the ground is crucial—it determines how strong the plant will be. Don't rush the process of letting things grow in your life.

WHAT IS THE GROUNDWORK YOU NEED TO LAY FOR YOUR GARDEN TO FLOURISH?

Two of my neighbors have large gardens. I pass them on my way to and from work. I'm always curious about what they've planted, and I wonder whose garden will produce the biggest, juiciest tomatoes. Aren't I silly to compare the size of a tomato from one garden to another as if we were in a competition? What really matters is that we share a love of gardening.

Comparing ourselves to others is a losing proposition. There will always be someone smarter, more skilled, and more talented than you are. Always. The minute we compare ourselves with anyone, we end up on the losing side.

IT IS EASY TO LOOK AROUND AND COMPARE WHERE YOU
ARE IN LIFE WITH OTHERS. DO LIFE YOUR OWN WAY;
BE PATIENT. EACH GARDEN IS DIFFERENT.

KINDNESS

Kindness is like snow—it beautifies everything it covers.

KAHLIL GIBRAN

Acts of kindness don't need to be planned and are often spontaneous. The other day I stopped off at the grocery store and saw a young mother who'd finished unloading her cart. I offered to return it to the store and was surprised by how grateful she was for such a simple act of kindness. It doesn't take much these days to be a bright spot in someone's life.

IT RAINS A LOT IN THE PACIFIC NORTHWEST, SO WE NEED TO MAKE OUR OWN SUNSHINE IN AS MANY CREATIVE WAYS AS WE CAN. BE THE BRIGHT RAY IN SOMEONE'S DAY.

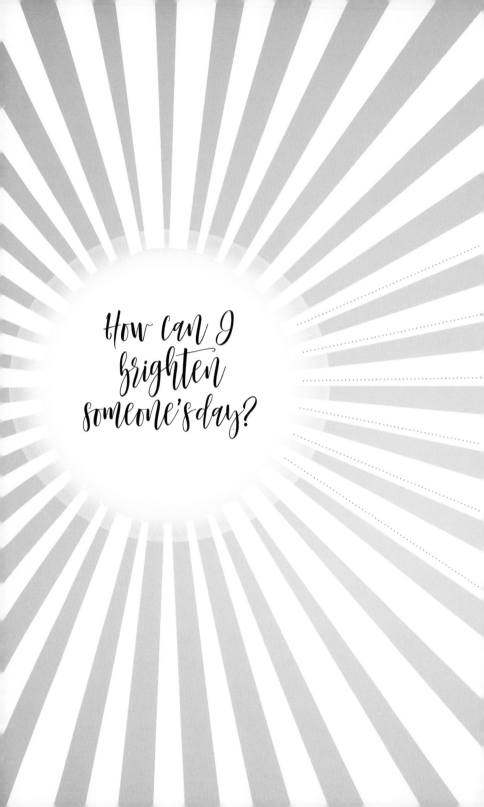

How can I brighten someone's day?

BE AN ENCOURAGER. SCATTER SUNSHINE.
WHO KNOWS WHOSE LIFE YOU MIGHT TOUCH WITH
SOMETHING AS SIMPLE AS A KIND WORD.

*Too often we underestimate
the power of a touch, a smile,
a kind word.*

LEO BUSCAGLIA

WHAT ACTS OF KINDNESS HAVE MOST IMPACTED YOUR LIFE?

Our words matter. They are impactful. I have learned from being an author how true this is. Making sure we are thoughtful in what we say to others is a way to ensure we are being kind.

A useful tool for being thoughtful in what we speak is practicing the pause. Pause, and be certain you are choosing your words wisely and carefully.

When she speaks,
her words are wise,
and kindness is
the rule
for everything
she says.

PROVERBS 31:26

THINK OF A TIME WHEN SOMEONE WENT OUT OF
THEIR WAY TO SHOW YOU KINDNESS. HOW WERE YOU BLESSED?
HOW DID YOU BLESS THEM IN RETURN?

Goodness

Goodness is an attribute that I try to consciously grow in my life. Goodness for me means "uprightness of heart and life." It encompasses your full character—your morals and ethics, your generosity and fairness, how you live your life toward others.

This brings to mind one of my favorite angels, Shirley, from my book *Shirley, Goodness and Mercy,* who said: "But remember, we're angels, not saints." I'm certainly no angel, just a human, and none of us are saints, either. But in our day-to-day walk, we can choose goodness. We can choose to live an upright life and to have a good heart toward others.

Every person has only one purpose: to find perfection in goodness.

LEO TOLSTOY

HOW CAN YOU SHOW GOODNESS TO OTHERS?

Giving back

Organizing a dinner for the Teen Center

Opening and reading all my reader mail

Delivering a meal to a neighbor in hospice

New plots that will encourage and inspire my readers

Expressing thanks for small or large gifts

Serving my community

Sending knitted items to World Vision, a humanitarian organization that supplies these knitted items to children in need around the world

FOLLOW MY EXAMPLE AND CREATE AN ACROSTIC
POEM FOR THE WORD *GOODNESS*.

G ....

O ....

O ....

D ....

N ....

E ....

S ....

S ....

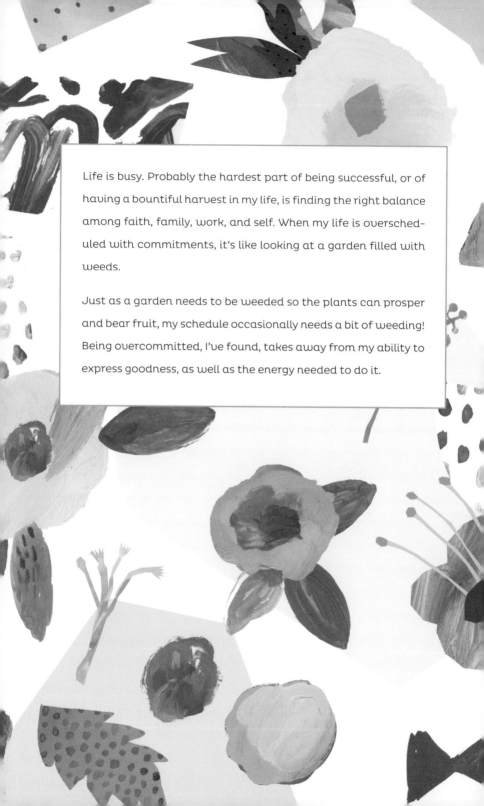

Life is busy. Probably the hardest part of being successful, or of having a bountiful harvest in my life, is finding the right balance among faith, family, work, and self. When my life is overscheduled with commitments, it's like looking at a garden filled with weeds.

Just as a garden needs to be weeded so the plants can prosper and bear fruit, my schedule occasionally needs a bit of weeding! Being overcommitted, I've found, takes away from my ability to express goodness, as well as the energy needed to do it.

WHEN YOU PUT YOUR LIFE INTO FOCUS,
WHAT IS IMPORTANT TO YOU? WHAT WAYS CAN YOU ALLOW
YOURSELF TO FOCUS ON GOODNESS?

WHAT NEGATIVES IN YOUR LIFE
CAN YOU TURN INTO POSITIVES?

How far
that little
CANDLE
throws his beams!
☀ SO SHINES ☀
a good deed
in a
naughty
WORLD.

WILLIAM SHAKESPEARE

The more we find ways to express compliments, the more rewards we will harvest as we see the happiness that sincere and genuine praise can bring to others.

Like plants that spread their roots underground to start new life, our words can help to spread goodness to others. Fill these clay pots with words of encouragement as roots for growth.

Good,
the more
communicated,
more abundant
grows.

JOHN MILTON

I love hearing from my readers, so in every book, I include my mailing address. And most people don't believe it, but I read each and every letter I receive. They are like fertilizer to my soul, to my heart, and to my work. Hearing how a certain story has been a reassurance to a struggling woman, or how a certain character touched one of my readers' hearts . . . Those letters sustain me to keep creating and writing.

A simple note, a thank-you card, or a thoughtful letter can have a profound effect on a person's life.

WHO ARE THE PEOPLE IN YOUR PAST OR PRESENT
YOU CAN REACH OUT TO WITH A NOTE OF THANKS,
A SIMPLE "I'M THINKING OF YOU," A CHEERY UPDATE,
A LETTER OF ENCOURAGEMENT, OR EVEN AN OFFER
OF RECONCILIATION? WHAT WOULD YOU SAY?

When I think about growing goodness through generosity, what comes to mind first is the ancient story of the widow's mite. In this story, an impoverished widow donated her last two mites, coins worth only a few cents. She gave all she had with humility, sincerity, and without drawing attention to herself. This was in extreme contrast to the wealthy men in the story, who were arrogant, superficial, and flamboyant in the giving of their much larger donations.

The widow's offering was far superior to all the others, for it was all she owned, and she gave it in faith and with a genuine heart. We don't need a lot of money to be generous. All of us can find ways to express goodness to others.

In a world of
self-centeredness,
we are called to be
extravagantly
generous.

I'm inspired by my readers on a regular basis to
spread goodness through generosity.

We all have tools and gifts—which we can use to help others.

THINK OF WAYS YOU CAN USE YOUR TALENTS TO BE A BLESSING
TO OTHERS—LOOK FOR THINGS THAT DON'T REQUIRE MONEY.

The teens at my church put on a dinner to collect money for missions. Tables were marked with flags from various countries around the world: the United States, Spain, China, Costa Rica, and Thailand, to name only a few. Wayne and I were seated at a table bearing the flag of a small African nation.

When the food was served, our table of eight was given a bowl of rice to share and a bit of fruit to pass around the table. Those seated at the USA table next to us had platters of food delivered to them: fried chicken, rolls, vegetables, and apple pie.

It was an object lesson I'll never forget. We have been given so much in comparison to others around the world. How can we *not* be generous in our giving to others in need?

Faithfulness

My tomatoes, green beans, and varieties of squash depend on me to give them the attention needed to grow and to produce fruit.

Faithfulness is a fruit that is so important in our lives. Faithfulness says to others: "I will keep my word. I will not fail you. I won't quit on you."

Let love and faithfulness
never leave you; bind
them around your
neck, write them
on the tablet
of your
heart.

PROVERBS 3:3

WHO IN YOUR LIFE DEPENDS ON YOU?
WHO EXPECTS YOU TO KEEP YOUR WORD,
TO BE TRUSTWORTHY, NOT TO QUIT?

Faith in action is love.
Love in action is service.

MOTHER TERESA

REFLECT ON HOW THIS QUOTE SPEAKS TO YOUR LIFE.

....

....

....

....

....

....

....

....

....

....

Keeping promises is an integral part of the fruit of faithfulness. Even when I get exhausted from life—my responsibilities and the commitments I've made—I must keep going. I've found it important to be a woman of my word.

A
faithful friend
is a strong defense;
and he that
hath found him
hath found a
treasure.

ECCLESIASTES 6:14

Faithful friends are important to me. They depend on me, and I depend on them. I have a friend who I can count on to be completely honest with me, a friend who shares my deep love of knitting, a friend who continually reminds me to take care of myself, a friend who is ready to be my prayer warrior, and a friend who I can call at any time of the day or night if I need a listening ear. My friends are the trellis in life—they hold me up, make me stronger, and protect me.

WHO ARE THE FRIENDS WHO HOLD YOU UP IN LIFE?

....

....

....

....

....

....

....

....

....

....

....

....

....

HOW DO YOU SHOW YOUR FAITHFULNESS TO THEM?

....

....

....

....

....

....

....

....

....

....

....

....

....

Some of you who have followed me for a long time know that Wayne and I host our grandchildren for what we call "Grandma or Grandpa Camp": a week of spending time with them.

At least once, I had an offer for a promotional tour during a scheduled Grandma Camp, but I turned it down. Another time, I fell behind on my writing schedule and was tempted to reschedule our week. But no, I had made a commitment to my granddaughters, and I was going to keep it. I knew I needed to model faithfulness by keeping my promises. Through modeling it, I recognized that I was teaching it. If someone can't trust you, you lose credibility in who you are. This is an important lesson to be learned.

*Your patient
love and faithfulness
may be exactly what
they need to complete
a turnaround.*

JOYCE MEYER

WHO IN YOUR LIFE IS WATCHING YOU CLOSELY?
FOR WHOM DO YOU NEED TO MODEL FAITHFULNESS?

WHAT COMMITMENTS HAVE YOU MADE
THAT YOU NEED TO KEEP?

WHO IS SOMEONE YOU SHOULDN'T GIVE UP ON?

....

....

....

....

....

....

....

....

....

....

....

....

....

Gentleness

Nothing is so
strong as
gentleness.
Nothing is
so gentle
as real
strength.

SAINT FRANCIS DE SALES

Gentleness is sometimes equated with being soft, weak, or submissive. I've found that not to be true at all. Gentleness is, quite simply, the most powerful force in the universe.

In early spring when I see the tender sprouts peeking through the garden soil, I tread carefully to avoid accidently hurting one of them. I know that although these small starts look weak, their roots are strong, and they hold the power to create a bountiful crop.

DO YOU SEE GENTLENESS AS A

STRENGTH OR A WEAKNESS? WHY?

DO YOU HAVE ANY PEOPLE IN YOUR LIFE WHO EXHIBIT A GENTLE
NATURE? HOW CAN YOU MODEL THEM?

I've found that gentle people aren't reactionary. They don't respond immediately. They have an inner strength to choose if, how, and when it is necessary to respond.

CAN YOU THINK OF A TIME WHEN YOU WOULD HAVE BENEFITED FROM BEING LESS REACTIVE?

Be a rainbow in
someone else's cloud.

MAYA ANGELOU

I avoid putting poisonous chemicals in my garden. I'd rather use vinegar instead. Words are like poison when they are intentionally meant to hurt others. And they do hurt. While they might not cause us to bleed, they can create injuries. Sticks and stones do hurt, but then so do words. Keep the poison out of your garden and out of your relationships for an abundant harvest.

Have a heart that
never hardens,
and a temper that
never tires,
and a touch that
never hurts.

CHARLES DICKENS

HAVE YOU EVER REACTED TO SOMEONE NOT REALIZING WHAT
BATTLES THEY WERE FIGHTING? IT IS TRUE WHAT IS SAID, THAT
EVERYONE IS FIGHTING THEIR OWN BATTLES.

Self-Control

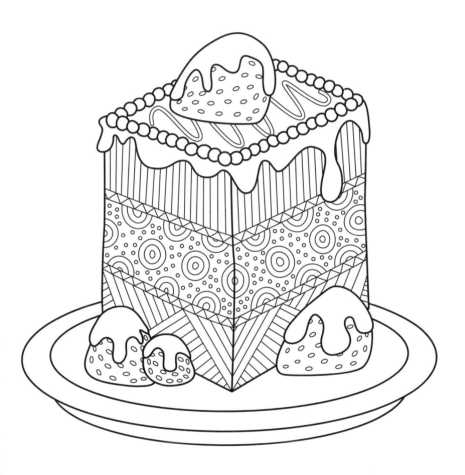

God gave us His Spirit.
And the Spirit doesn't make
us weak and fearful. Instead,
the Spirit gives us

POWER

and

love.

He helps us
control ourselves.

2 TIMOTHY 1:7

I add 2 Timothy 1:7 to my signature when signing books. Sometimes I will have a line of five hundred people waiting for me to sign their books and take a picture with them, which equates to several hours and a very sore hand. But I make the time to add this after my name in hopes that someone may wonder and look it up and be encouraged. Maybe that small gesture will spark growth in another.

I'm a swimmer. For more than thirty years I've set the alarm for 4 a.m. so I can finish my reading and journal writing before I head to the community pool. This is my way of staying healthy. To have a good harvest you have to give nourishment to each part of your life. Often I'm tired and long for an extra hour or two of sleep, but this habit is deeply ingrained in me, and I'm grateful. The advantages of getting in my laps have reaped more benefits than I can count.

TRACKER

EXERCISING ○○○○○○○○○○○○○○○○○○○○○○○○○○○○○○○
HEALTHY EATING ○○○○○○○○○○○○○○○○○○○○○○○○○○○○○○○
QUALITY SLEEP ○○○○○○○○○○○○○○○○○○○○○○○○○○○○○○○
MAKE NEW FRIENDS ○○○○○○○○○○○○○○○○○○○○○○○○○○○○○○○
FIND A NEW HOBBY ○○○○○○○○○○○○○○○○○○○○○○○○○○○○○○○
FLOSS YOUR TEETH ○○○○○○○○○○○○○○○○○○○○○○○○○○○○○○○
WEAR SUNSCREEN ○○○○○○○○○○○○○○○○○○○○○○○○○○○○○○○
DRINK LOTS OF WATER ○○○○○○○○○○○○○○○○○○○○○○○○○○○○○○○
TAKE A DAILY WALK ○○○○○○○○○○○○○○○○○○○○○○○○○○○○○○○
_____ ○○○○○○○○○○○○○○○○○○○○○○○○○○○○○○○
_____ ○○○○○○○○○○○○○○○○○○○○○○○○○○○○○○○
_____ ○○○○○○○○○○○○○○○○○○○○○○○○○○○○○○○
_____ ○○○○○○○○○○○○○○○○○○○○○○○○○○○○○○○
_____ ○○○○○○○○○○○○○○○○○○○○○○○○○○○○○○○
_____ ○○○○○○○○○○○○○○○○○○○○○○○○○○○○○○○
_____ ○○○○○○○○○○○○○○○○○○○○○○○○○○○○○○○

I'M doing
THIS
For ME

Grit and self-control
are strongly correlated,
but not perfectly so.

ANGELA DUCKWORTH

Sometimes there's an overabundance of opportunity, a row crowded with too many seedlings that need to be thinned out. It takes self-control to find the right balance among family, work, and service, and it's not an easy task. I've found that for every yes, I find a gentle way to say "no." It can be difficult, but it's necessary to our health and to strong relationships.

LIST THE THINGS YOU CAN SAY NO TO AND THE THINGS YOU
SHOULD BE SAYING YES TO THAT YOU ARE NOT.

Guard your time
fiercely.
Be generous with it,
but be intentional
about it.

DAVID duCHEMIN

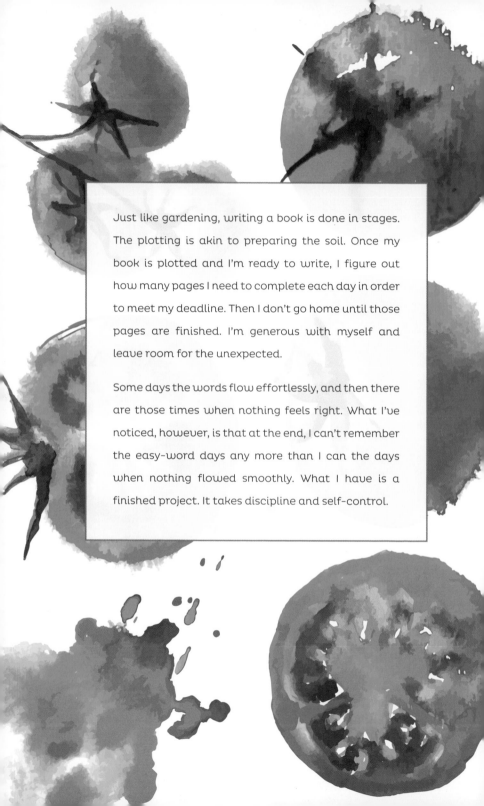

Just like gardening, writing a book is done in stages. The plotting is akin to preparing the soil. Once my book is plotted and I'm ready to write, I figure out how many pages I need to complete each day in order to meet my deadline. Then I don't go home until those pages are finished. I'm generous with myself and leave room for the unexpected.

Some days the words flow effortlessly, and then there are those times when nothing feels right. What I've noticed, however, is that at the end, I can't remember the easy-word days any more than I can the days when nothing flowed smoothly. What I have is a finished project. It takes discipline and self-control.